copyright 2012
Originally published by Kingston Publications 2008-2011
ISBN-13: 978-0986691102 ISBN-10: 0986691100

ACKNOWLEDGEMENTS

I'd like to thank Tracy Weaver, Donna Kearns, Sarah Moore, Jane Deacon, and all the folks at Kingston Publications.

A shout-out to Audrey Webb for her incisive editing and to the brilliant Wendy Treverton's design and layout. Special love to brother-husband, Doug and sister-wife, Danielle, who have opened their heart and homes to me and my family more times than I can count.

Most of all, I devote this book to my kids, Brendan and Laurel, fellow artists whose commitment to their passions inspire and amaze me. And finally to Gus, the cutest dog I've ever owned. I would've mentioned you first, darling, but the others would've gotten jealous.

FOREWORD

Humans tell stories. It's what we do. It helps keep us sane. Cows don't tell stories and look how mad they went for a while.

The five years during which I wrote these particular stories were a time of great loss and great renewal. I went from being young to over the hill, from a helicopter parent to an empty nester. From married to single, single to pathetic, and pathetic to a woman who finally learned how to be on her own after forty years of having to be with a man. I forgave my mother and even slow-danced with her on a Saturday night. I laughed deeper than ever before and I cried so much that God should've put windshield wipers on my eyeballs. After days of alternating between feeling great and dissolving into a puddle on the sidewalk, I started to find a new strength and confidence I never knew I had. My friends called it post-menopausal zeal. Or maybe it was post-menopausal meal. I'm not sure; I was too busy wailing to hear properly. In five years, I had to rewrite the press release I had issued about myself. Trying to create a new story hurt like the devil, but I found that if I stayed open and teachable, the universe showed up with casseroles and a good story, both of which will keep you warm on a cold night. I hope you will enjoy these tales of ho and ha and will laugh at me. And also with me, because we're all in this together, so we might as well share a good laugh. Besides, you're not getting any younger and someday you'll be in a nursing home and no one will want to be your roommate if you're complaining all the time.

that Which doesn't kill

you makes you Funnier

IT TAKES A VILLAGE TO RAISE A NEUROTIC

"i explored the power of now, like there was no tomorrow."

For years I've gone from pillar to post trying to improve myself. I was under construction so much, I needed a building permit.

I'm always in search of the next DVD, class, or book. By the way, have you ever noticed bookstores never have a self-improvement section for men? There's no book called *Men Who Love Too Much*. Men tend to fix things, not people. They tinker with engines, not personalities.

But me? I did everything. I envisioned prosperity. I got my colours done. I found out what colour my parachute was. I explored The Power of Now like there was no tomorrow. It wasn't enough to improve just myself — I motivated everybody I met. I motivated my hairdresser so much he became my landscaper. Instead of trimming my bangs, now he trims my bonsai.

My kids didn't escape my self-improvement frenzy either. I dragged them from harp and piano lessons to soccer practices and games. I was trying to improve their genetic lot in life, so I enrolled them in French Immersion. I can't speak French. Some of my relatives don't even speak English that well. But I wanted my kids to be bilingual. Now I can't understand a word they're saying. After all that sacrifice, they ran away from home without even saying good-bye. Or if they did, I didn't understand them. They should come with subtitles.

I was left alone, all by myself, in the empty nest that I had to clean because I motivated the cleaning lady so much she was in med school. I'm hoping she'll support me in my dotage because the kids aren't going to be able to. (What do you call a performing arts student with a Bachelor of Arts degree? Living with your Mom. The Sequel.)

Maybe I am getting older, or maybe all this self-help helped, because now I am making friends with my vices. I accept my weaknesses more quickly. In fact, I do all things too quickly. My Tai Chi instructor says I move so fast it looks like I'm disco dancing. As a survivor of the Donna Summer era, I take that as a compliment.

Enough already. I've decided that maybe my house is finally in order. I may need a coat of paint here and there but it's too much effort to rewire myself. I don't mean to be motivational about this, but if I can accept myself, so can you. Go into the bathroom right now, take off your clothes and look in the mirror and say, "Hey, I might as well love this body the way it is, because ten years from now this one's going to look pretty darn good." Do that a few times without puking, and then try it with the lights on.

After all, you are a diamond in the buff.

PATCH ADAMS FANS, UNITE

"believe Me, When you stand buck-naked outside the hospital, they bring the drugs right out to the street."

On the sixth day of January, I had my first epiphany. I decided to be a better person — a person who helps.

I had recently turned fifty and figured that since I was getting older, I had better start cramming for my finals.

I was sick of just writing checks for charity and buying cheese from the schoolkids. I wanted hands-on helping, like maybe saving children from warlords in Africa. So I went to a local café to ponder how I could get started. I ordered fair trade coffee but the barista told me they didn't have any. I sat there drinking my four-dollar, unfair trade caramel macchiato, thinking about all the things I would do to help the downtrodden, when a guy sat down beside me. He was playing a very noisy game on his cell phone. I tried to ignore him and focus on what Bono or Bob Geldof would do in this situation. And then I got thinking, "Which one is cuter? Bob or Bono? Bob? Bono?"

Hot men. Hot coffee. Hot men. Hot coffee. And the guy kept beeping his phone and I was getting ticked off, so I started doing a chant I learned at hot yoga. Namaste, I said under my breath. Bless him.

Beep.

Bless him.

Beep.

BEEEEEEEEEEP him.

Beep.

Finally, I turned to him and said, "Will you please SHUT UP!" Okay, I didn't really say that, because I am a people-pleaser. And what if he didn't like me? But I did start to question how I would ever deal with African warlords if I couldn't handle a few beeps from a cell phone.

This existential pondering caused me to have a serious anxiety attack. No, I have that backwards. I thought I was having a heart attack, called 911, and when I got to the emergency room and saw the waiting time, then I had the anxiety attack. I got labeled "urgent," which isn't nearly as fast as it sounds. I sat there so long that someone asked me if I was

5 PATCH ADAMS FANS, UNITE

an organ donor.

After four hours, I met Amiel, a blue-haired woman wheeling a silver coffee cart. Amiel on Wheels. She was living proof that the heart of any hospital is the volunteers (and maybe the cardiac surgeons). She was the quintessential volunteer. Over a couple of Peek Freans and some water thinly disguised as coffee, she informed me that she had joined the hospital volunteer team during the Korean War. It was two dollars a year for her membership and she did it only for the free volunteer luncheon. Over her career as a volunteer, she said she'd come to love helping others. Sadly, she confessed, she had seen many changes in charity work over the years. It was getting harder and harder to help people, she said, what with more germs, more fears, and more rules.

For instance, since the advent of the Privacy Act, she isn't allowed to tell anyone outside the hospital who's staying there. That's crazy! Think about it. Why would an eighty-five-year-old woman risk breaking a hip if she couldn't bring back a little gossip to the seniors centre?

I don't know if it was Amiel or the forty percent oxygen I was huffing, but my breathing finally settled. That's when I had my second epiphany. I wasn't supposed to go to Africa. Sure, I was to think globally, but I had to act locally. I was being called to be a hospital volunteer. Of course, I could never work in the emergency ward, not where people are bleeding, or complaining, or throwing up. Puking makes me gag. And I'd never help with patients; I can't sing Christmas carols or sponge-bath dirty old men. No, I couldn't do that, but I could use my humour. I could be Patch Adams. I could make jokes in the coffee room with the First Response Team. (Which are cuter: cops or paramedics?)

In a flush of excitement, I announced my intentions to Amiel and in a second her face turned to stone. She looked like I had just announced the bus trip to Branson, Missouri had been cancelled.

She hissed at me, "There is at least a six-month waiting period."

"Six months?"

"Volunteering is not just helping out, you know," she declared. "We weed out the fickle ones. The high school kids who want a form signed. The cons doing community hours."

"Amiel, I haven't done time," I defended. "I live on Amherst Island."

"How do you think they populated Australia?" she retorted. "There's due process. You have to have a police check."

I started fantasizing about a cop patting me down and said, "Amiel, they can do a cavity search for all I care. I haven't been able to get in to see a doctor in months."

She didn't crack a smile. I could see she had never heard of Patch Adams.

"Look, missy, this red apron is not given out to just anybody," she said. Then she sold me a 50-50 ticket and wandered off to spread her bad coffee and whitener to other unsuspecting sick people.

I checked myself out. As I was leaving the hospital, a very disturbed woman stormed past me, and the security guard, whose head was the size of a turnip, picked her up and put her out on the sidewalk. All she wanted was her meds. That woman might have been having a bad day, but one thing is certain — she is more resourceful than I am. She stood out in the ambulance bay and took off all her clothes. Believe me, when you stand buck-naked in the hospital, you get service. In fact, they bring the drugs right out to the street for you.

That's when I had my third epiphany: It's as hard to get good service as it is to give it. I went home, wrote a cheque to Bono, and binged on the cheese order I had just gotten delivered from the schoolkids.

ALWAYS A BRIDE, NEVER A BRIDESMAID

"i won't go to candle parties because i don't like people knowing what scent i use."

What do you call twenty-eight women sitting in the living room spreading melted brie on rice crackers, pounding back cocktails, and yapping like crows sitting on a fence?

If you said a Tuesday night book club meeting, you'd be close. The answer is a bridal shower for my cousin Francine's daughter, Helen.

It's been a custom for decades now to shower new brides-to-be with things that will help them set up a household. But most brides today have either lived on their own and collected their own trousseau, or, in Helen's case, have been down the aisle more than once. That being said, this time around Helen has had a household shower, a teacup shower, and then the one I was invited to — a boudoir shower. Since she's on her third marriage, I think Helen needs a frequent flyer card for a divorce lawyer, not another pair of chocolate underpants.

I don't like boudoir showers. I won't go to candle parties because I don't like people knowing what scent I use, so I have no interest in opening paraphernalia for intimate relations. I wasn't a complete party pooper. I bought her an over-the-shoulder boulder-holder that lifted and separated, which Helen would likely be doing soon.

Amidst the hot pot stickers and mini quiches, I thought about how showers have changed. As a young woman, I remember the speech I gave to my mother: "If you ever give me a bridal shower, I will boycott it." I hated the crustless sandwiches, and that brides had to sit in a wingback chair with streamers of pink above their heads while somebody made a hat out of a paper plate and bows. Now everybody drinks. We didn't have hooch back in my time because broads didn't booze it up in front of their mothers. That and Auntie Vera had just gotten back from the Betty Ford Centre, so there was a punchbowl of mocktails — two cans of pineapple juice and an antabuse chaser.

When I got married, I wasn't registered anywhere. I wouldn't dare dictate what gifts should be given. My aunts gave me family recipes and a nice piece of Pyrex and some cookie sheets. I know brides today don't want cupboards full of junk, but getting a horrible gift or two is part of the fun. You won't remember perfect flatware choices, but a pink lady toilet paper cover is a great story waiting to be told. A story like that will keep you company when you're old and in the nursing home.

Men often say some women play games. That statement is no truer than at a bridal shower. There are two kinds of people: people who like to play shower games, and the rest of us. There is always some game-playing harpie who is screaming at everyone else, "Stop being party poopers! Making a pot scrubber into a doll is SO fun."

It isn't fun. Nor is it fun to see how many clothespins you can get off a clothesline with one hand or trying to get a hotdog that's tied around your waist into an empty Coke bottle.

For a while, feminists tried to boycott the games. They wanted to act like men and hire a stripper. Believe me, it isn't fun having a guy called Long Dong Silver dance in front of you to "Love to Love You, Baby" on a boom box. You don't know where to put your eyes and it's never pretty when your mother starts disinfecting the leather couch.

I did find one shower in thirty years quite fun. We were asked to dress up in the ugliest bridesmaid dress we had ever worn. I remember Helen had to borrow one of mine because she had never been asked to stand up for anyone. Always a bride, never a bridesmaid, apparently.

At that shower, Auntie Vera was the hit of the afternoon. She wore her honeymoon negligee with Marabou fur slippers. When we whistled at her like construction workers, she quipped, "I was pure as the driven snow when I got married. Why, I walked down that church aisle, I said a few vows and that night I was supposed to be as hot as a firecracker. It was no First of July, I'll tell you that. More like April Fools'."

No matter how the games and customs have changed, the free advice hasn't. Every family shower, we offer the bride-to-be words of wisdom on how to stay married. Except for a couple of us, most people are still married in my family because "til death do us part" isn't an idle threat to them, it's a promise.

Here are a few samples of the *bon mots* flowing on Helen's special day:

"Never let the sun go down on your wrath."

"If you killed him, you'd get only twenty-five years, but marriage is a life sentence."

Auntie Vera, who had taken up drinking again in 2002, took the prize for the most maudlin words of the day: "Appreciate your man while he's alive because before you know it, you'll be old and he'll be dead and you'll be eating beef jerky from a bag wishing you had someone to yell at."

Soon after, the afternoon drew to a close. I decided to take Auntie Vera home with me. Last time she went back to the nursing home in that condition, she almost got kicked out for feeling up an orderly.

I kissed Helen good-bye. "Maybe third time's a charm," I said. And Vera slurred, "Yeah, maybe the horns in his head will match the holes in yours," but Helen had that far-off look all brides-to-be have, like they're soldiers going back to Afghanistan for a third tour of duty.

When I got home, I tucked Vera under the blanket on the couch. I sat munching leftover egg salad sandwiches and realized that the main thing that has changed about bridal showers is *me*. I actually like them. Not because of the gifts or the party games, or even because I still believe in happily ever after, but because except for funerals, it's the only time I get to see my relatives.

At that moment, Auntie Vera exhaled a loud snore followed by a long period of silence. Thoughts flew through my head. *Oh my God, what if she's dead? I'll need a new outfit. I hope the relatives will fly up from the States.* After about thirty seconds of mind chatter, she inhaled once again and her rumbling snores drowned out the sound of a westbound train.

FINANCIAL INSECURITY

"Never let people know you have cash lying around, or they'll want to borrow it."

I wake up in the night thinking about money. Some people count sheep; I add up what I will have to live on each month when I turn sixty-five.

Like a lot of people, I didn't save as much as I should have. See, I didn't plan to live this long. To paraphrase the Black Sabbath song, "Dying young was my financial plan." So was buying lottery tickets and waiting for my ship to come in.

The latest plan has been waiting for relatives to die. (Rich relatives, I mean. Who wants poor ones to croak? Their families would likely ask me to raise money to bury them.) What would be the harm in some nasty, rich relatives that I've felt morally superior to all my life croaking and leaving me some cash? I know what you're thinking: Why on earth would people I've harboured contempt for my entire life leave me moola? Simple: They want to buy my love. And I'm okay with that.

But what would I do with all that dough? Money has confused people since back in the day when we were using beads as a form of payment. So, just in case one of my wealthy relatives kicked the bucket, I decided to gain some knowledge. I went to the bank for financial advice. This is a lot like asking a pharmaceutical rep if they think antidepressants are a good idea.

If banks know one thing, it's how to make money. I got some lovely help from a financial advisor who has asked that her name not be mentioned in this essay. Mum's the word, Bynthia.

Like all financial planners, Bynthia has that chart. You know that chart they like to pull out and tell you that if you started saving a hundred dollars a month when you were twenty-one, you'd now have $850,000? I used to think they pulled out that chart to rub my nose in how pathetic I am. But now I realize they don't want me to get my hopes up. That chart makes me cranky. I always want to scream, "What kind of person starts saving a hundred bucks a month at twenty-one? A cheapskate, that's who!"

My cousin Jack saved, but nobody wants to be him. He's so cheap that when he opens his wallet, the Queen squints. Moths fly out crying, "Go to the light!" Jack was the one that always owned Park Place in Monopoly. He learned to play bridge at twenty-one. I, on the other hand, played strip poker, and I always lost my shirt.

Jack got some strange messages about money. He was taught to sock it away for a rainy day. He's always talking about the bottom line. To me, money has never been the bottom line. Children are the bottom line. Quiet children who won't beg me to buy them stuff at the mall.

My messages around money were a series of contradictions: Work hard so you can be rich and retire early. Rich people are snots. Never let people know you have any cash lying around, or they'll want to borrow it. The other message was always to buy the best, but make sure it's on sale. The best sentence you can say in my family is, "And not only that, it was thirty percent off!"

These messages are complicated, but join two people in holy matrimony and a new set of problems arises. It seems there are two kinds of people in a marriage: the spender and the saver.

In some cases, two spenders marry each other and find they don't want to spend on the same thing. I was an artist. I spent cash on art classes for the children. My husband liked equipping the house with boring things, like sump pumps.

This resulted in the "shopping-at-each-other" phenomenon. This is where one person buys something the couple can't afford and the other one says, "I'll show you and I'll buy something we can't afford, too." And then they both hide the items, and when the credit card bill comes in, they argue about whose fault it is that they're in the mess they're in.

Some couples seem to guarantee that their money can never be pleasurable. Two of my friends went out to buy a vehicle. He wanted a sports car. She wanted a minivan. They bought a truck. That way nobody was happy.

Money controls our moods most days. My friend Reid used to say his serenity was based on his bank account balance.

Anyhow, according to Bynthia and her chart, for the balance of my life, I would need to be on a financial diet. I nodded my head at her like this was really going to happen. It was the same nod I used to give the skinny broad at the Weight Watchers meeting who said I should eat less. That diet usually lasted as long as it took me to get to the nearest McDonald's drive-through on the way home.

After I left the bank, I went down to the harbour and watched my ship pass me by. As I was sitting there, I thought about how I may not have as much as I want, but really, I have a lot. In fact, I have spent my life on a lot of great experiences. And these experiences will make me a rich and sought-after speaker when I hold court in the common room at the seniors centre, which is where I'll be camping out because I won't have any cash for an actual room.

And after that, unless Cousin Jack wills me a lot of cash, I will be cremated and tossed out to sea. And as tourists see parts of me floating by in Portsmouth Harbour, I hope they'll say the same thing about me as they did when I was alive: "That chick has a great ash."

TO KISS OR DOUBLE KISS? THAT IS THE QUESTION

"It's a regular hugging frenzy, a real hug-o'-war."

The handshake has fallen out of favour because of viruses.

In its place, there seems to be a lot of people doing the double-kiss — a gaggle of revelers who insist that if you kiss them once, you are going to have to turn the other cheek.

This is how it goes. You say hello and move toward the person, perhaps kissing them on one side of the face, and then just when you're about to move on to the next person, they pull you back in for the second smooch. Sometimes the greeting takes longer than the entire conversation. Frankly, it feels contrived — affected, really — but when I expressed my concern to one partygoer, she said, "Dahling, the double-kiss is *so* Montreal." She said it with a British accent, which proves my point. She's from Napanee.

To prevent you from making the same social faux pas I have, here are some of the latest trends for the seasoned greeter:

1. People from Toronto hug.
2. People from Montreal double-kiss.
3. People from Montreal who do yoga double-kiss and double-bow.

Double-kissing has also leaked into the business world. I travel a lot for work. Once I went to Montreal and later in the same week, I was in Toronto. During a momentary lapse of memory, I forgot which city I was in, leaned in and double-kissed my perspective client — right on the smacker. I turned red and said, "It's *so* Montreal." Suffice it to say, I got the job.

My point is the double-kiss does not belong at work. Can you imagine Donald Trump saying, "It's a done deal; we

17 TO KISS OR DOUBLE-KISS? THAT IS THE QUESTION

double-kissed on it." In fact, in some businesses the double-kiss means the deal's off, and when you get home there'll be a horse head in your bed — lest we forget *The Godfather*.

The reason I'm protesting double-kissing so much is because I had just gotten the whole hugging thing down. I had learned to hug just the right amount of time, not too tight, not too long. I had learned to put down my purse so I could do it with both arms. People have actually said, "Deb, you are a good hugger." Others have said, "You can let go now; you're acting like a stalker."

But it is a miracle I can hug at all, given where I come from. My people are a repressed tribe; we're Irish. It's not that body contact is repulsive to us — we love a good bar fight — but we don't go around touching people when we're sober. When I was growing up, if a woman embraced you, she was either burping you or performing the Heimlich manoeuvre. Some of the most tender moments of my childhood were when I had a piece of gristle lodged in my windpipe.

Then a few years ago, it all started to change in my family. I blame it on my sister, who went on a walking tour of Italy and fell in love with a lovely Italian fellow named Mario — and as a result of that inter-affectionate union, hugging became part of the norm. Like the ubiquitous spinach dip, it began showing up at every family event. We are now hugging at birthdays, baptisms, funerals, and reunions. It's a regular hugging frenzy, a real hug-o'-war.

Relatives you never liked because they were from *that* side of the family are now hugging willy-nilly. This is totally confusing as far as I'm concerned. If you give hugs to relatives you don't like, how will they know they've been written out of the will?

Random hugging like this starts to feel forced. It has no meaning, a lot like the standing ovation. People in this country stand up for anything. A Grade Three student's harp recital of "Twinkle, Twinkle, Little Star" doesn't actually *require* you to jump to your feet and yell "Bravissimo!" Half the time, I'm not sure if the audience likes the performance or they're trying to beat the rush in the parking lot.

Whether we shake hands, hug, or double-kiss, I just think we should all get on the same page. Whatever we decide, it should reflect the times we're living in. With the onslaught of global warming, maybe it's time handheld fans come back into vogue. Not those handheld electric jobbies, but the old-fashioned fan, like the ones from a Jane Austen novel. We could all sit coyly on the divan and flutter fans back and forth in front of our faces. The problem is, at my age, people might not know if I was saying hello or having a hot flash.

BOOMERANG-BACK BABY

"If you love something, set it free; if it comes back, it's probably an... adult kid needing cash."

This year, my kids came back for a stopover. Some friends said I was asking for trouble by weakening my perimeters, but I was thinking of my retirement. When I get old, my kids will have to reciprocate and let me come stay with them. You may call that emotional blackmail, but I call it financial planning. With the current economy, I'm on the Freedom 55 plan; I'll retire when my kids are fifty-five.

I wasn't an empty nester without borders. I had stringent guidelines. They couldn't go to the bathroom in the middle of doing the dishes — I had fallen for that one for ten years. There were to be no extracurricular activities in the bedroom, unless they brought someone home for Mama.

What's the harm of having kids back at home? There was a time when it was customary for young people to live at home until they got married. Farmers. Italians. Cultures that knew enough not to kick kids to the curb, especially not when they were still of use to their parents. Back in the day, the role of adult kids was to make sure Mom and Dad would never have to be in the same room together. Talking about their kids' latest stunts bonds a couple. Once they're gone, what is there to chat about? Golf handicaps? The remains of their RRSPs? The latest episode of "Grey's Anatomy"? That's how my marriage ended. During the TV writers' strike, the kids moved out and we were left in a room together pointing a remote at the TV with nothing to say.

People say they like having their space back, but in the old days, there was no space. People lived in three-room farmhouses and had to share a bed with four other people. With the current energy prices, that might not be such a bad idea — think of the money you'd save! Less than a century ago, they had less space and people turned out okay. Now we have 1.5 kids and 2,500 square feet of house and we feel crowded if the fruit of our loins is camped out in the rec room.

Many also argue that kids need to be independent, but we forget that they've been in daycare since two and had their own key to the house since they were five. We even cancelled Grade Thirteen so they could get through school faster. And just because they're not under your roof, doesn't mean they're not asking for cash.

Now, I know they can return for too long. My cousin Francine's daughter boomeranged back pushing a baby carriage before she'd even reached legal drinking age. Francine has a kid with a kid in the basement and her aging mother living in the spare room. Poor Francine is on call 24/7, sandwiched between three generations of people who want her to wait on them. There are endless doctor's appointments for knee replacements for her daughter. Apparently they gave out after too many childhood soccer games. The other night Francine was up until three in the morning giving dating advice to her mother, my Aunt Marjorie, who is seventy-six, but apparently still has a lot Romeos sniffing around in the seniors centre.

I had my two kids return under my roof for a very limited time. There was a definite shelf life to our reunion, but I found out what good people they had become. As twenty-somethings they were actually nice to me. In fact, I believe it's far worse for *teenagers* to live at home. Kids should move out when they're fourteen and come back when they've stopped sighing and saying "whatever."

When my kids moved out again, I realized I liked thinking of someone other than myself. I get weirder and weirder living on my own. I have started making small things into big deals. I could run a small country on the energy I am now putting into cooking and cleaning and my animals. At Christmas, I bought myself a pet, a dog named Gus. He's a Shih Tzu I got from the pound and, because he had fleas, he was shaved in the back. He looks like Kurt Russell with a reverse mullet: party in the front and business in the back. I brag about him. I have 346 pictures of Gus — more than I took of the children. Every morning I tell him, "Go out to the kitchen and make Mama a cup of joe." Yes, he sleeps with me but he isn't allowed on the couch. It's crazy; I used to leave my real kids with babysitters I'd just met, but with the dog I'm running background checks on the kennel to make sure they don't have any priors.

At night I sometimes pretend he's Lassie from that the old '50s TV show. Lassie knew if people needed her help. Lassie would go and find them in the well. So I say to Gus, "Go get the kids. Tell them Mama needs them back home with her. Go, boy! I think one of them has fallen into $25,000 worth of student loan debt and needs his Power Rangers bedroom back."

Gus is cute, but not that bright. He just stands there staring at me, then walks around three times, gets up on the pillow, and goes to sleep like he doesn't understand a word I'm saying.

NAVIGATING LIFE ON THE INFORMATION HIGHWAY

"We have just enough information to be dangerous."

Last year, I cancelled my satellite television.

I convinced myself I would read novels by authors like James Joyce. It's 365 days later and I'm still on page one of *Ulysses*, but I have cut my sleeping medication in half.

I've traded staring at the TV screen for staring at the computer screen. If I'm not sitting at it, I feel empty. I stare lovingly at it waiting for pop-ups. I worship it. I have become a checker. I check endlessly.

This is how my day goes. I get up and go to the coffee shop for a cup of anxiety and free Internet access. I check LinkedIn, my eBay account, Zoomers, and Craigslist, and then read the news online. The news is so bad I read it again on another site just to make sure it really is that horrible. Who needs terrorists when the media terrorizes us on a daily basis?

Then my mother calls and tells me I'd better batten down the hatches as there is a hurricane coming up the coast of Costa Rica. We're scared of weather. The weather is now news. And news is now sport. It's confusing.

After I hang up the phone, I notice a lump on my index finger that I'm sure wasn't there when I got up, so I Google my imagined illness du jour. I surmise that I have either a malignant tumour or gnarly knuckles. We have just enough information to be dangerous. I don't trust my doctor or my financial advisor but I trust an online site to reflect the state of my mutual funds. Thinking I know how to do my own financial investing is like thinking I can do my own Pap test.

At this point I need something to stop the increasing fear, so I go online to check how many points I have on my fifteen rewards cards. I have so many passwords, I fear I will lose my mind one day and be sitting in a nursing home saying "rascalsbum343." If you want to check your income tax online, Revenue Canada now makes you create your own security questions. This means I don't know the answer or the question. Don't you love it when the customer service people start giving you hints? "Your first dog's name mixed with Grade One teacher's name?" Mittens Woodly, which sounds like what I'd call myself if I was a porn star.

What I need is human contact — a little Facebook to Facebook. I have 499 friends; 349 of them are Kimmetts who are talking about how much they've been drinking. At least they won't blow over the legal limit driving on the information highway. Facebook is to social media what the smoking section was to high school — people yakking about nothing and feeling cool doing it.

I know some people will say there is more to life than balancing a computer on my legs all day doing the laptop dance. I mean, I didn't grow up on devices like Crackberries and iPhones. I am so old, I remember when the phone rang and I used to pick it up. Now I stare at it and say, "Ah, great. Why is he calling me at this time of night?" and I let it go to voicemail. Then when he doesn't leave a message, I think, "What kind of game is this guy playing?"

There is only one thing worse: when you call your phone and that woman's voice says, "You have no new messages." Then she says it again. "I mean it. You have no messages, loser." I hate her and I hate that gal at Bell Canada — Emily. I am pretty sure Emily was my dental hygienist — the one who loved getting the big puppet out and telling me I hadn't been flossing — before she got that job at Bell Canada.

I take a time-out. I bow my head and do the Blackberry prayer. If I don't text, do I exist? If a tweet falls in the forest, does it make a sound? I have been reduced to short-form replying; I spell when I could speak. I type TTYL to my BFF but I refuse to write LOL. I'm old-fashioned. I say ha ha. Or hee hee. For someone with gnarly finger syndrome, I have the fastest fingers in the west.

Regular texting is bad enough. Add a man to the mix and everything happens ASAP. I met a man online. At first it was innocent enough, just spelling back and forth, LOLing our fingers off. I didn't think I was going to be his e-mail-order bride or anything, but I had no idea it was going to get textual. I mean, so textual I had to light a cigarette after I pushed the send button. It's called sexting. I was such a tease. I'd "sext" him for fifteen minutes then leave him with a dangling participle. I should have gotten his credit card. After my fifteen minutes of shame, I decided to be celibate. I put my phone on vibrate, stuck it in my pants, and called myself over and over again.

As this year starts, I've gone back to watching TV. No, I won't sign up for satellite. I will now stream everything I really like. My virtual world is my own new reality show. It's like that old saying: "The geek shall inherit the earth, or at least the World Wide Web."

CHEATING EVOLVES INTO "HAIR"-OWING EXPERIENCE

"blame it on bed-head or boredom, but i found myself cheating on my hairdresser."

Let me start by saying I love my hairdresser.

For seven years, she was a faithful and loyal stylist. Let's call her Rhonda, because if you call her Ronny she goes Sweeney Todd on your head.

Rhonda and I have been together since the early 2000s, when she convinced me that maybe it was time to get rid of my Farrah Fawcett hairdo. She told me the curling iron was dead. And she didn't just cut my hair; she was more like a therapist. We shared medical stories. Showed each other our surgery scars. We read *People* magazine, and questioned why Sheryl Crow ever dated Kid Rock or Lance Armstrong. We were comfortable.

But then things started to slide. Rhonda got more successful and I became a road warrior, spending more time on the highway than I did at home, and, well, I started looking around. It was innocent at first. I was eyeing other people's up-dos. Their de-frizzed hair. Rhonda started making me wait longer for appointments.

One night I was out of town, alone in a hotel room, and I had an overwhelming urge to get my hair cut. Blame it on bed-head or boredom, but the next day, I found myself in a salon called "Pretentious." The walls were black and silver and trendy, and the owner was an angry hair barista named Ovid. His face had so many tucks, he looked like either Siegfried or Roy, whichever one was attacked by the tiger.

But boy, Ovid was good. He knew how to use a pair of scissors. From the moment he slung the bib around my neck, I knew we were in for a dynamic and tumultuous ride. He asked daring questions: "Are you dramatic or attractive?" I said, "I'm both," and he kissed me on the cheek and laughed. He began swinging his paintbrush around my head, madly swishing and swashing colour this way and that. But as he was dolling me up, he was also insulting me, telling me my lipstick was horrid, my clothing colours were all wrong and my last hairdresser sucked. If we had been in a reality show, it would

29 CHEATING EVOLVES INTO "HAIR"-OWING EXPERIENCE

have been called "Hostile Makeover."

Some people, if attacked by a hair-orist, would storm out. But not me. No way. In fact, I tipped him more than I normally tipped Rhonda — twenty percent. I also bought products. Lots of wax and glue, straighteners, and volumizers. The more he insulted me, the more attached I got and the more I bought. Why? Because I'm as conceited as the next woman, and when it was over and done with, he made me look fabulous. Everybody said, "MY GOD, WHERE DID YOU GET YOUR HAIR DONE?" (Yes, they said it in capital letters.)

So for the next four months, I snuck around behind Rhonda's back again and again and again, driving to another city to see Ovid. I couldn't get enough of the guy, but then he started to get crazy. In fact, he was dangerous. "Cross your legs again and I'll cut your ear off like Van Gogh" kind of dangerous. Talk about temperamental. If I didn't *love* what he did, he sulked, and frankly the cuts and colours were getting crazier with every appointment. The last time I left looking like a skunk.

My friend Lorna, who doesn't sugarcoat things, lit up a smoke and blew a plume in my direction. (Some call it second-hand smoking. I call it smoking for free.) "It's your own doggoned fault," she said. "You cheated on your hairdresser. It's instant karma. Just add water."

She was right. And I had to be honest with myself. It wasn't the first time I'd cheated. The only reason I started seeing Rhonda was because Melissa was out on maternity leave. And to be really, really honest about it, Melissa wasn't the first service person I had stepped out on. My cleaning lady was the first. I didn't like the way she did things, so rather than tell her, I brought in the Molly Maids on her off-week. She caught me when she found a dirty Swiffer cloth in the laundry room.

"What's this?" she accused, veins popping from her neck.

"Maybe I was dusting."

"What kind of fool do you take me for?" she sniped back.

"The kind that wants symphony tickets. Box seats?"

It was then that I realized it was time to stop this behaviour. I had one more chance to change, to do it right. But what was I going to tell Rhonda? How could I say that I had gone somewhere else? I couldn't pretend I was a victim of a random drive-by colouring. After all, I looked like Pepé Le Pew.

We started slow. Built trust. I brought her a coffee from Tim's. I bought cheese from her kids' school and raffle tickets from her husband's hockey team.

The first cut was the deepest. I am not mincing words. After my first cut back with Rhonda, I looked a little like Edward Scissorhands had had his way with me. Then, instead of using the usual foils to colour my hair, she inflicted the colouring cap on me. It's an old-school bathing cap they put on your head, then use crochet hooks to pull strands through microscopic holes, often leaving tears in your eyes and dents in your skull.

Now, Rhonda and I are back together. We have settled once more into a nice routine. That's not to say I'm not tempted. I walked by Ovid's shop the other day when I had occasion to visit his city again. There he was, looking out the window, smiling. It wasn't because he was happy; he was wearing a chin strap. Must have had a nip and tuck. I considered going back to Ovid. I even went to dial his phone late one night, but then thought better of it. A person who went back to that kind of pain would have to have holes in her head. ∎

SHORT STORIES

"they look like the Wicked Witch of the West. Warning 'i'll get you, my little drug dealer. you and your little pit bull, too.'"

It's summertime and the living should be easy. Time to ignore all your problems — stick your head in the sandbanks.

Summertime — time to get outside and enjoy the sights. I'm a people-watcher, and every year, I marvel at the young women strolling by in their shorts. Shorts so short they could double as car chamois.

Personally, I haven't worn shorts in decades. I've never felt the need to push my bottom into a pair because, from the rear, it looks like two puppies struggling to get out. From that angle, it looks like my cheeks are chewing bubble gum.

Now listen, I'm not putting myself down. I'm very grateful for the legs I have. They go all the way up to my waist. They are decent, stocky, Irish peasant legs, meant to support me as I carry rocks up a famine hill. I'm fine with that. This year, I lost a lot of weight — 175 pounds. Actually, 172 were my ex-husband, but still, those three pounds were brutal. But as thin as I might get, I've finally accepted that my legs will never grow longer.

The reason I don't care much for shorts is not because of the size of my legs, but the colour. There is none. I don't tan. Like paint chips, there is white and there is French white and linen white. But mine are white white. I have zero pigment. When I sit by one of those SAD lights, they cure my depression but give me sunstroke.

Refusing to wear shorts has held me back in life. I could never be a nudist. Other nudists would go snowblind. I could never be a postal worker. Dogs would take one look at my Bermuda shorts and immediately want to bite me. I could never be a cop. Cops are forced to wear shorts. Was it not bad enough they put them on bikes? How humiliating it must be for them, wearing Bermuda shorts and cycling like little demons, chasing bad guys driving souped-up, vibrating cars. They look like the Wicked Witch of the West, warning, "I'll get you, my little drug dealer. You and your little pit bull, too."

My self-imposed shorts ban started back in my childhood. As a teenager, I was the one at the beach always pretending I'd forgotten my bathing suit. "I'll just wear my Levis." Not cut-offs. Full-length jeans. And boy, those suckers get heavy when they're wet. It's a wonder I wasn't found at the bottom of the quarry. One time I wore pantyhose under my bathing suit, and when people came up to me and said, "Hey, you're wearing pantyhose," I did what any self-respecting person would do. I denied it. "Uh, excuse me, I can't help that my legs get darker at the top," I lied. "And these webbed toes? Well, duck feet run in the family."

And so did bad taste in shorts. Thinking of some of my relatives who wore shorts gives me bad dreams. I still have nightmares about Cousin Garney bending over trying to start an outboard motor, a cigarette hanging from his mouth, gas leaking everywhere . . . and not from the motor. He used to wear shorts with black socks and penny loafers. He would be decked out in his short shorts, the kind with no net pouch. Outright commando, if you get my drift.

I can be walking along a street in the dead of winter and suddenly get a flashback of Grandma Mary wearing her pink hot pants and blue pantyhose with white shoes. To church. She'd go up the aisle every Sunday flirting with the men who took up the collection. She always insisted on travelling to the beach in the same getup. For those road trips, she'd also sport her massive sunglasses and jam cotton balls in the side in case rays of sunshine tried to sneak in. In those days, there was no air conditioner in the car, and she would never let me roll down the window because she was afraid she might gulp wind. Apparently, if you gulp wind, you could blow up! That, and she didn't want to get dirt in her hair. Okay, not her hair, her wig. She had no real hair of her own. She had a closet full of wig heads. If she ever sent you in there to get something, it always seemed they were talking to you.

I don't want to inflict that visual on the younger generation. So I sit here in my Mrs. Roper caftan that I got at Value Village, grooving to the sounds of Edgar Winter. For some reason, I feel a kinship to the man. Compared to me, he looks tanned.

ADDICTED TO OIL

"I have a bamboo yoga suit. When i sweat, i smell like a burmese...... Forest."

My last name being Kimmett, I was called Kermit a lot.

Like the Muppet, get it? I hated it as much as you can imagine. But as I get older, I realize Kermie was a lot wiser than he looked. For instance, he advised, "Never fall in love with a pig." Think of how many hours of pain you could have avoided if you had only listened to *that* one!

He also said, "It isn't easy being green." You got that right, Kerm! In fact, it isn't easy smelling green, either. I have a bamboo yoga suit. When I sweat, I smell like a Burmese forest. Saving energy can be exhausting. I began using compost worms. You think cats are fussy? Worms won't take your garbage unless you've ground your kitchen scraps in a blender. (Note to Cousin Francine: I *told* you that wasn't a smoothie.)

I use cloth bags for my groceries. Or at least I intend to. I still haven't gotten them from the car to the grocery store, but I still say no to plastic bags. No matter how many groceries I have, I stuff as many items in my handbag as I can. I've gone through three purses so far. I'm reducing plastic, but increasing leather consumption. The cows may be mad, but there are fewer of them passing wind.

I am also in touch with garbage. Where I live, we have no curbside pickup. Our garbage men are called husbands. After my husband got voted off the island, going to the dump became my responsibility.

The first time I had to go there, I thought maybe I should have tried harder to make my marriage work. The whole experience of going to the dump is a way of increasing lung capacity. My lungs got so strong, I could buy my "pay-as-you-throw" tickets, have a chat with the attendant, Dr. Love, unload a month of garbage, and not breathe until I got out to the main road.

I have also gotten in touch with the seedier side of life. The feral cats roam the place like deadbeat dads. So do retired men. Women may go to the washroom in pairs, but men go to the dump in packs. (Considering what happens in both these places, maybe there isn't that much difference between the genders after all.) The guys stand around, casually talking trash by the heap of rotting garbage, their bellies hanging over their belts. With guts that size, they may be recycling, but they're sure as hell not reducing. Even so, I've noticed they do look a lot younger than men who don't frequent the dump. There's a lot of wind out there, and if they stand in the right direction, it pulls back their wrinkles, making them look like they've just had a Botox treatment.

But you have to watch these slumdog millionaires or they'll start bringing home treasures. Ladies, I can tell you from experience, if that happens, you must treat your fellow the way you would a cat when it lays a dead mouse on the welcome mat. Scream at them: "Get that *thing* out of here!"

Conservation can be a complicated issue. Dr. Love told me that his doctor told him to get off trans fat. I asked, "Why don't you get off salad, because that lettuce travels 1,500 miles to get here?" The cost of oil is going up but it's still the cheapest substance on the planet. You can put four people in a car and drive four blocks on a cup of gas. You can't get a rickshaw driver for that.

Let's face it: We're addicted to oil. We're powerless over the fossil. I don't know how to get off it, which source of energy to use. I've got a gas fireplace, an oil furnace, and a propane stove. I check the paper every day and use the one that's cheapest. I got a Smart car because it's supposed to be energy efficient, but it's like American beer: I can't get a head on it. I drove by one of the wind farm turbines and the Smart car got sucked up. Where I live the only "green shift" is what the cormorants leave all over the front lawn.

   The government's solution to any addiction is to levy a tax. They get us hooked on smokes and booze, and when we can't live without them, they tax us. We need to go to a twelve-step program. Our leaders need to be sponsors — be the power of example and go to the ethanol clinic with us — because, as addicts, we make promises we can't keep. Like when my kids were little, I said I wasn't going to use disposable diapers, but I wasn't committed. I kept a spare pack around just for travel, then just for the park, then just for the middle of the night. Before I knew it, I was up to three packs a day.

   No longer can we bury our heads (or our garbage) in the tar sands. We need visionaries who will have the creativity and courage to lead us into a new way of doing things. In fact, I think we need more females in power. We could use menopausal women as an alternative heat source: We could plug our fingers into a generator and refuel the heating panels at night. We're not sleeping anyway. Of course, you'd have to remind us why we were in the furnace room in the first place. We'd probably get the heat going then get a power surge and scream at the cat, "Take that fur coat off! You're making me hot just looking at you!"

   No matter what the solution to our energy woes is, it's going to take courage to stick to it. It's not easy being green, but it's even harder being yellow. ■

SAY HI TO AUNTIE CAMPING

"For god's sake, get the Mosquitoes off my winky!"

The heat of the summer makes us do crazy things.

A friend of mine called me last week and asked me to go camping. This is a new friend, one who doesn't know my stance on camping. She obviously didn't get the memo. She's the fitness type — does hot yoga four times a week. You know hot yoga, where they crank up the heat and you're forced to do the downward dog in 150-degree temperatures? It's like paying for a hot flash.

Anyhow, this yogic friend thought I was an outdoorsy person. I look the type. I have a Kellogg's Corn Flakes face. People take one look at me and want to take me on a hike. Living on an island doesn't help. People think that if you live in the country, you must like gardening and baking apple pie. They're half right. I like to watch people garden while I eat pie.

I hate camping. Camping is evil. My idea of roughing it is when I check into a hotel room and discover there is no room service.

I have never outed myself on this subject before, mainly because camping advocates are like golf fanatics, who think you're kidding when you say you have no desire to walk around an eighteen-hole golf course in the heat of the day, trying to get a ball into a little hole. They consider it their personal mission to convert you.

The first lie camping advocates tell you is that it's so peaceful out there in nature. Actually, nature is bloody noisy: all that wind, the grackles and crows getting up at the crack of dawn. Why is it that all the ugly loud birds have to get up early and squawk outside *my* tent?

And sound carries near the water. You can hear everything people are saying and doing. A campground is a bunch of gassy people packed together like sardines. It's like going to the suburbs, but with a longer commute.

Camping aficionados try to put a spiritual spin on it by saying it's good for the soul. Really? You will not find camping mentioned in any of the world's good books: not the Bible, not the Koran, and not the Talmud. Not one of these books mentions camping as part of the soul's development. In fact, the Jews had a word for camping — exile.

Still, my soul did give camping the ol' college try. I have kept diaries illuminating the many times I've attempted to commune with nature after nightfall.

Take this excerpt from my diary, when I was age nine: "Dear Diary: Beneath the twinkling stars, as we picked gray ash off our marshmallows, Mom gave me heck for using starter fluid to light the campfire. She assures me my eyebrows will grow back eventually."

Or how about this one at age eleven: "Dear Diary: During daylight hours, the Girl Guide tent seemed to be pitched on flat ground, but as the night wore on, I found I was on the wrong end of the slant. The blood rushed to my head; the air mattress slowly leaked air until it was one flat pancake. And there, at the Sandbanks, was that one and only rock, which lodged itself in my back, doing permanent kidney damage."

Age seventeen: "I thought that after all the lemon gin, I'd pass out. I have black fly bites all over my tuckus from losing sixteen games of strip poker. Spent most of the night heaving over the three-seater commode."

At around twenty-eight years of age, I stopped trying. But then I got married and had kids, and one summer day, my husband said we should go camping. It would be a fun family holiday, he said. He knew about the tent ban; it had been part of our prenup. It was written that we would never attempt camping, wallpapering, or shopping together at Ikea. But somehow he managed to convince me to give it a try — he's a golfer. We made our way to the wild woods, this time renting a tent trailer.

What is it about a musty smell and centipedes that gets a man in the mood to try something exotic? In the throes of passion, he started spanking — himself. Don't think it didn't ruin the mood when he started screaming, "For God's sake, get the mosquitoes off my winky!" As we sat basking in the glow of calamine lotion, he wondered if the neighbours had heard us through our soundproof canvas walls. "No, honey," I assured him, "I'm sure it was sheer coincidence that those nice men came by on their four-wheelers singing the theme song to *Deliverance*."

I know it may sound a bit grandiose, but I believe I am the chief activator of violent climate change. If ever I was camping on a beautiful sunny summer day, surprise tornados and flash floods would appear out of nowhere and devastate a provincial park within minutes. So I have stopped camping, for my sake and yours. But like a bad lover, I've given camping one too many second chances. The only "sole"-full thing I have ever experienced while camping was cleaning doo-doo off the bottom of my Crocs. Apparently bears *do* shit in my neck of the woods. ■

HOLIDAY GIVING: LIVING IN THE PRESENT TENSE

"I'm more of a drive-by shopper. I get in and get out. I don't linger."

Last year, on the twenty-fifth of August, my cousin Francine swished into my house with her Christmas shopping list.

The back-to-school stuff had not yet been slashed. The Halloween goodies weren't even on the shelves, yet there she stood, her credit card aimed and ready to swipe. She informed me that time was a-wasting. It was time to go holiday shopping.

"Do you want to go in on the gifts this year or do you want to go by yourself?" she asked. "You know how you get at this time of year."

Francine and I love each other in that blood-is-thicker-than-water type of way. She, however, can't stand that I don't like shopping. I'm not a mall-town girl like her. At this time of year, I get present tense. I'm more of a drive-by shopper. I get in and get out. I don't linger. But she browses. Ruminates over everything. She starts collecting next year's gifts the day after Christmas. When I say "stuff," I mean "twee," which is a British word that means "junk" (with a British accent, it sounds better). A few examples of twee? Frilly potpourri angels. Ring holders shaped like high heels. Potato chip bag clips decorated with rhinestones.

When you open twee, two questions automatically pop into your head: How long do I have to keep it before I can re-gift? and What category of recycling would it go into at the dump?

Francine loves her twee. She can't go anywhere without it. She arrives at every house for supper with a beeswax candle or a jar of something she just made or saw on The Shopping Channel.

Francine's twee obsession has gotten worse over the years because she's trying to emulate Martha Stewart. I love to hate that woman. No wonder she ended up in jail — just to give us all a bit of a break. If I had shared a prison cell with Martha, I would have drawn mustard moustaches on her while she slept.

In my family, gift-giving has been a long and winding road. For a while, we bought gifts for everybody. But we're a very fertile family,

45 HOLIDAY GIVING: LIVING IN THE PRESENT TENSE

so it became too expensive. Then we started drawing names. Some people started complaining about the names they drew. And by "some people," I mean me. For five years running, I got Francine's name. I got her a hot-water bottle. Nymph Glands for your Lymph Glands. She already had one. Another time, I bought her a star. Not a twee star, but a high-in-the-sky star, one I could name after her. It came with a certificate, like a Cabbage Patch doll and at about the same price.

The constellation Francine is a woman running around tearing her hair out trying to find stocking stuffers, because that was Francine's next bright idea. We all got a stocking full of small things. I suggested leaving the credit card bill in so people would know you spent double the amount that you would have on a really good gift.

Next, Francine introduced the game where could steal each other's gifts. You know, the one where you unwrap the present and then the next person in line can take it away from you? Now *there's* a game for people with childhood issues. Inevitably, we'd all be teleported back to 1966 when Cousin Jack stole my Malibu Barbie. He had said Santa wanted him to have the doll and me to have the western log house. I should have let sleeping logs lie, because when we were playing the game last year I pointed out that stealing gifts might not be in the spirit of the holidays, causing Jack to leave in a huff. At least I got to keep the napkins he had his eye on.

Finally, we did something sensible. We agreed that Francine and I would do what we do best. She could go to the States for a day of shopping and I could go online for a day of Googling. It was exhausting, typing in that expiry date over and over again, but I stuck with it until my little fingers were about to fall off.

Afterwards, we got together and shared a cup of holiday cheer. A little eggnog and Red Bull to keep us awake while we figured out how much we owed each other.

"Now, you bought the Wii game so I owe you $46.98, which is in

American money. What is the dollar worth today? And the *Mamma Mia!* tickets were $138.50, so that makes it $13.25 less I owe you, but did you get the gluten-free shortbread from the Celiacs'R'Us website?"

In the middle of all the commotion, Francine handed me a card.

"I know we said we wouldn't get each other anything, but I saw it and thought of you. It's a gift certificate for a goat."

"You got me a goat?" That really got my goat.

"Not for you. It's for a family in a developing country. They get the goat and it helps feed them for a year."

"Wow."

"Do you hate it? I'm sorry. I can take it back."

"You can't give people a goat and then take it back. It's not the stealing game!"

"I mean I have a gift receipt."

"No, Francine. I love it. It's the best gift you've ever given me."

"Really?"

"Honestly, it's perfect." And I did mean it. In fact, I could feel my heart growing twee sizes that day.

Then a bell rang. Was it the fairy-wing wind chime she had given me last year? No. The festive cookies I'd squeezed out of a package were done baking. As I watched Francine chew and spit and sputter green dye and icing sugar in my general direction, I realized the old adage is true: You should never look a gift whore in the mouth.

THE OL' BAND AND CHAIN

"all of a sudden, every man alive or nearly dead became a prospect – at least to my newly naked finger."

A year had passed since my divorce but I was still walking around wearing my wedding ring.

It wasn't because I was sentimental or hoped for a reunion. In fact, the ring had been bought at a going-out-of-business sale, which should have been a clue as to how things were going to turn out. But one morning, it happened: I was out for a walk, having one of those imaginary fights with my ex — the kind that takes place in your head when you're giving him hell for that stupid thing he did in 1985. With very little persuasion, the ring flew off my finger and landed in a field of cows. Unlike the bovines, who appeared unmoved by this gesture, I felt liberated.

It turned out, however, that giving my ring finger breathing room unleashed twenty years of pent-up energy. All of a sudden, every man alive or nearly dead became a prospect — at least to my newly naked finger. At intersections, when a guy pulled up beside me, I'd give him the ring finger and smile before the light turned green. When that man would wave, nod hello or say, "Ma'am, could you please roll down your window and show me your driver's license," my left hand would sprawl across my cheek, showing off its little tan line.

When my accountant called to say it was tax season, I thought he said sex season. He does have a lisp, but I was beginning to freak myself out.

My friends said I was being ridiculous — a piece of jewellery did not have that kind of power. Obviously they'd never seen *The Lord of the Rings*.

I decided the only way to preserve my dignity was to retrieve the darn thing. But I couldn't start fishing for it in the cow patties. Not in daylight, anyway.

Out there in the dark, in my housecoat and a miner's light on my head, I learned a couple of things. One: Cows hump other cows. Two: My ring, much like my dignity, was irretrievable.

I realized throwing away my ring was like putting my house up for sale. Everybody who drove by was a potential purchaser, and it was a lot of work keeping my lawn cut and the bonsai bush trimmed. Let's face it, I'm lived in. I didn't want to keep everything fluffed and spotless all the time, and even if I could land a prospective buyer, knowing my luck, I'd end up with a loser who'd track mud through my "house."

The last time I was single, I was a twenty-five-year-old but my friends assured me this time around I would make good choices. In fact, they set me up with a few "good choices." They'd say, "Meet Harry, he's nothing like Larry," and I wanted to scream, "Yes, he is — except for the first letter, he's exactly like Larry!"

After several lapses in judgment (I kept going for renters, not buyers, if you know what I mean), the ring finger settled down. I realized my problem was that I thought my house was up for sale. But it wasn't, really. I was just in the process of cleaning out the closets, seeing what I wanted to keep and what I wanted to throw out.

When I am ready to entertain an offer, I'll be the one controlling the lockbox.

GONE FISHIN': INTERNET DATING REELS IN NOTHING BUT BOTTOM-FEEDERS

"there is no such thing as an easy-going fifty-year-old woman."

It's hard being fifty. It's even harder being fifty and learning how to date again.

It was easier when I was younger. I could go anywhere. Now I have to go to places that have good lighting. When I was young, I was musical. I dated drummers. I am not trying to name drop here, but I dated the lead singer from Ambush. Correction. I exaggerate. I dated the singer from the cover band, Almost Ambush.

I saw him recently at the World Music Festival in northern Ontario and I realized that even if he had remembered me, I wouldn't be attracted to him at this point in my life. And it's not because he's bald on top or still has a mullet. Or that he's still driving a motorcycle . . . without a helmet. It's just that I heard him speaking and I realized I didn't know what he was talking about. All he did was talk in metaphors. He was a poet, and let us know it.

See, musicians are obscure. Take Bob Dylan, for instance. Would you be able to have a conversation with Bob? Or Leonard Cohen? I have fantasized about Leonard for years, but really, can you imagine living with him?

You'd say, "Hey honey, what do you want to do today?"

And he'd be, like, "First we take Manhattan and then we take Berlin."

"What? I thought we were going to the mall."

I don't just sit at home and think about unsuitable men for me during this period of my life. I think about unsuitable men in other eras, too. Who would want to hook up with Henry VIII? The eighth old man, I am Henry would have made me lose my head.

And Shakespeare? Speaking in iambic pentameter would be impressive for a while, but he'd always have ink stains all over his fingers.

What's really got me going on about this is that I did some Internet dating recently.

I was on the site plentyoffish.com for a while. For people not plugged in, I'm not joking. There really is a site by that name; the regulars

51 GONE FISHIN': INTERNET DATING REELS IN NOTHING BUT BOTTOM-FEEDERS

know it as POF. They have a similar site for librarians called plentyofmicrofiche.com. You don't use a password, just a Dewey decimal.

On POF, you post a profile letting people know what kind of person you are looking for in a relationship. For instance, you can say you want dating, chatting, or a long-term relationship. My favourite category is "Other Relationship." This is for cheaters who are making no bones about it. Check it out. Your current partner might be on it. Not that you could tell, necessarily. People create a pseudonym, or a handle, like on CB radios. Your moniker has to convey the right message. I was going to call myself "Who Says Flannel isn't Sexy?" or "Smells like Vicks VapoRub." I settled on "Too Old to Take Your Nonsense." They must have thought I was kidding because I got a flood of "you've got e-mails" from men I didn't even know I was looking for. It's a lot like shopping at Costco. You go in for mayo and come out with a year's supply of turkey.

The men on this site have a lot in common. They put pictures of their cars and their houses on their profiles. What's with the many heartbroken widowers carrying on about their dead wives? Talk about baggage! Yes, "Lost in Oakville," I'm talking to you.

And they all want a woman who isn't into head games. Where's the fun in that? They all want to take long walks. I already get enough exercise by getting up to go to the can forty times a night.

And they all want smart, easy-going women. FYI, fellas: There is no such thing as an easy-going fifty-year-old woman, at least one who's not in a coma.

And finally, men want sexy women. Right. The shirtless man with the C-cup breasts wants a sexy woman. Well, women want sexy, too. Online dating is a lot like the Sears Wish Book. We all want the Malibu Barbie, but sometimes what we get is a wool sock doll with buttons for eyes.

There are two ways friends react when they hear you're dating online. First they look at you like you're pathetic, with that look that says, "Has it really come to this?" Then they hug their husbands very tight and whisper, "Please never leave me."

They worry that you might meet a serial killer. The only "cereal killing" these men do involves a bowl of Corn Flakes every morning.

Once friends are assured of your safety, the second thing they like to report is that they know a couple who met and got married online. Okay, who *are* these people? What are their names and where do they live? Because, like the story about finding the rat in the fast-food burger, I think there was only one couple and only one rat, and it has grown into an urban myth.

How to assess who you want to meet was beyond me. At what point do you say, "I'd like to meet this man to whom I am texting. There's something about his well-placed exclamation point. Only a sensitive, caring man would choose a font like that."

I guess I became a bit jaded. I thought I had something going with this one guy, and when we said we'd meet, I told him, "Look, if there is anything I need to know about you, please tell me now because I don't want to be surprised." And he said, "Not much. I'm on an iron lung. I am waiting for a double lung transplant. Do you mind?"

Do I *mind*? Of course I mind! Maybe I'm fussy, but I like my men to have both their lungs. It's called dating, not palliative care.

So I took my line out of the water and stopped fishing. I am happy just to spend my lonely nights listening to Leonard Cohen reminiscing about Suzanne.

But there is one man who still writes to me. So far, it's really quite romantic. His moniker? "Life without Parole." So far, it's working out very nicely.

LIVE COMIC WALKING:
MY TOUR OF A FEDERAL PRISON

"there are so many dos and don'ts when touring a Maximum-Security Facility."

Most people can go their entire lives and not feel the need to tour a prison, but I'm writing a movie about prison guards.

Female prison guards, to be precise. I got interested in female guards because I am in comedy. In the world of comedy, men outnumber women about ten to one and I was interested to see how women coped in another primarily male-dominated system. As I started doing research, I quickly found not only that there's a high percentage of females working in corrections, but that a good deal of them guard men. We all guard men in one way or another, especially after a few cocktails, but I was surprised. After countless interviews, I realized I needed to visit an institution if I was going to be able to reflect the culture.

I thought about going into Quinte Detention Centre, but there would've been too many of my relatives in there wanting me to bring them smokes. So I booked a tour in Millhaven, which is very simple, really. Like five degrees of separation kind of simple. I must admit, I had no idea what to expect. There wasn't a brochure. No pictures. In my imagination, I thought it would likely be worse than a Kimmett family reunion, but not as bad as when my hometown lost a hockey game.

Yes, I am joking. I use humour to deflect fear. The more freaked out I am, the more jokes I make, then three days later, I feel my real feelings and freak out. So the day I went into The Clink, I was hilarious, cracking jokes about what I should wear. Sporting a rack like I do, I don't want to set anybody off, having the boys overcome by an avalanche of lust. (Yes, they were bad jokes.)

In the end, I opted for a loose sweater and jeans with a gel bra (because the underwire one could be used as a shiv). And then, to top it off, I put on four pairs of underwear, which I know logically wouldn't have saved me, but it might have slowed things down while the big-necked officers came to save me.

As I drove up the driveway, the first thing I saw was a sign that said "Trespassers will be prosecuted and can spend up to five years in jail." This is when I hoped they had received my request for the tour. When

LIVE COMIC WALKING: MY TOUR OF A FEDERAL PRISON

I got to reception, I was greeted by my tour guide — a former female guard. She didn't have a thick neck. In fact she was kind of, well ... short. And very pretty. So I said, "Boy, you're short," which went over as well as you can imagine. And that was just the beginning of the stupid things I did and said that afternoon.

There are so many dos and don'ts when touring a maximum-security facility. Don't wave at the guys with the guns in the tower. It makes them nervous. At security, don't ask if they can check your IUD while they're doing that body search. Don't pet the drug dog. Just smile and let him sniff your crotch. Don't be worried that he'll bite you. He's a drug dog, so he's probably getting off on the smell of your J'Adore cologne. In fact, don't wear J'Adore cologne to a correctional institution, because it won't be just the dog sniffing you.

Don't make small talk with the guys in jeans and T-shirts. They are inmates. They don't wear carrot suits in federal. Yes, I said "carrot suits." I know the lingo. And don't say "carrot suits." You sound like an idiot. When you see inmates wearing jeans that hang low like plumber's butt, don't say, "For God's sake, pull your drawers up and get a belt," because cons can't have belts. And don't call them cons. They might just be murderers or bank robbers, not con artists. And speaking of art, when you see ink drawings of Medusa all over a guy's arm, don't say, "Hey, love your 'too. What gang are you from?" And don't ask, "Are you holding?" Not even as a joke, because some chicks might suitcase drugs up their woohoo, but you're not that kind of gal. Besides, you're old enough to be their mother. Or grandmother. The inmates at Millhaven are younger than you'd expect. A lot younger.

When you see the cells, which are painted pale pink, blue, and green, don't say, "Who the hell picked out these paint colours? Did Martha Stewart get loose in here and make them paint it the colours of Whoville?"

When I go anywhere, I develop an accent. Two days south of the Mason-Dixon Line, and I'm saying "Y'all want some grits, y'all?" Within sixty minutes of being in Millhaven, I was developing a swagger and spouting lines like "Guard or cons, we're all doing time. The only difference is I get to go home at night."

And then I started comparing my job as a humourist to theirs. "Oh, you were part of a hostage-taking? That's nothing. I worked with Mike Bullard."

Just because I "died" on Mike's show, it's not the same thing. That metaphor won't fly, because being a woman in corrections is front-line feminism. Some psychologists claim women are a calming influence on men. The concept is that a tough guy sees a woman, he'll just be struck peaceful. He'll fall into some estrogen-induced form of narcolepsy. (And if she has PMS, he'll voluntarily put himself in solitary confinement.) I don't know how it works. I do know that anyone in a uniform is seen as an authority figure. And authority is what everybody in there is bucking against. So, everybody has to find a unique way to survive. To be seen as human or not to be seen at all. It's a delicate balance for women. And the ladies I met were tough, funny, and very serious about doing their jobs well. But here's the thing: Working in corrections, whether female or male, is not an easy job. It makes that gig I did for the Buffalo Tow Truck Operators look like a picnic.

After my hour-and-a-half tour, I was released. As the gates opened, I yelled, "Live comic walking!" and everybody thought I was a riot. But three days later, the jokes stopped. I heard on the news that a guard had shot one inmate for trying to kill another. I finally got that I don't have a clue how you walk off a day like that. I don't know how impending violence plays on a psyche day after day, year after year, because I am not a guard. I am a comic who gets to go home at night. And hopefully, never go back in.

CIGARETTES, MOTHERHOOD, AND ZOMBIE ATTACKS

"he'd lift me up while screaming in a scottish accent, 'how many stone are ye, woman?'"

A few weeks ago, I had just finished telling someone how nicely my son had turned out.

How he was quite the lovely young man, how he's grown up and no longer visits with friends wearing only his boxer shorts, how he's stopped scratching body parts at the dinner table, how he's stopped asking his girlfriend to pull his finger. I was saying how good he is with money and how he can make soup. A man that can make soup is a good man. No sooner had the words left my mouth when he came back home — and on the same weekend that he'd decided to quit smoking. I do want him to quit, believe me. I wish he'd never started. But he was trying to quit in my home, on an island, without the patch, without gum, and without bringing me a three-day supply of Atavan.

For the first day or two, he slept and ate and said it was good to be able to breathe again. Then there was the deep-breathing phase, and the breathing turned to yoga — he started doing strange bird poses in the middle of the living room. His leg would unexpectedly swing behind him. He walked in the woods, happy as Snow White — I expected to see little bluebirds flitting around his head. As he started feeling better, he began lifting weights — me. Without any warning, he'd lift me up and try to bench press me while screaming in a Scottish accent, "How many stone are ye, woman?"

As the nicotine leached out of his system, the emotional outbursts started. Think of the terrible twos except with a terrible two-year-old that could bench press you. He was like someone who had Tourette's. He would just started swearing and freaking out for no reason. *No, I don't want to do the dishes. No, I don't want to go to bed. No. No. No.* But not as cute as a two-year old you could distract ... or knock out by slipping a Gravol into his sippy cup.

Then the cranky stage got replaced by the ridiculous question phase. The following exchange is a sample:

"Mom. Mom. Mom. Hey, Mom. Was I a bastard? "

"No, son. You certainly were not a bastard."

"But you and Dad had to get married."

"We didn't have to get married. We chose to get married."

"Because you were having a baby."

"No, we had you and then got married. Remember I told you I had to breastfeed you in my wedding gown?"

"I see. So, I was born out of wedlock?"
"Well, technically, yes."
"So I am a technical bastard!"
"What, are you from the '50s? You're not a bastard. How many times do I have to tell you?"

The whole night was full of tangential bursts and non-sequiturs.

"Mom, tell me honestly. Do you think 'Ninja Turtles' was a better TV show than 'Power Rangers'?"

"I don't know. They were both better than that flipping 'Little Mermaid' we watched a million times. Where was that girl's mother? I'll tell you where. Dead."

"Mom, if you were forced to sleep with Sailor Moon or Pink Power Ranger, who would you pick?"

I said it would definitely be the Pink Power Ranger. Sailor Moon is under-age.

"Do you think Polly Pocket or My Little Pony was the worst toy ever?"

"Pogs were the worst toy ever, with Crazy Bones coming in a close second."

I made some supper and he ate half a side of beef, which I served on purpose. I thought all that red meat would put him into a drugged-out coma, but all that blood seemed to just wake him up.

"Hey, Mom. How would you survive a zombie attack? Would you shoot them with a gun, or stab them with a knife?"

Let me say, I don't believe in zombies. They are right up there with aliens as far as I am concerned. I don't think you should give aliens or ghosts or zombies any sort of encouragement. Because I'm sure it's like the law of attraction. If you start believing in them, they start believing in you, and before you know it you're in the psych ward because every time you see a meat thermometer you burst into tears.

By the way, the reason I knew about the zombie thing is from Facebook. In fact, when I YouTubed "How to Survive a Zombie Attack," I found many handy tips. And it has over 100,000 hits. Jane Jacobs' thoughts on urban sprawl and how we can survive as a human race has only 688. Go figure.

In honour of preserving the family relationship, I played along with the zombie thing.

"I'd kill the zombie with a knife because I don't believe in guns."

"That wouldn't work, Mom. Zombies have incredible lower arm strength and would take the knife out of your hand and you'd be dead."

"Then why did you give me the knife option?"

"I was testing you. I need to assess your chance of survival."

See, this is the thing about my son — he likes to have a plan. As a kid, he used to get up and demand to know the day's schedule. He always wanted rules, which I wasn't great at providing. I remember one day after I had been out for the night, the army called my house. The woman from the recruiting office asked for him.

"Is Master Brendan there?"

"No. He's at school."

"Well, he called last night about joining the army."

"He's in Grade Six."

When I asked him why he wanted to enlist, he said he needed discipline, and his father's and my methods were too willy-nilly for his standards.

So I knew if we were going to get any rest, we needed to get the zombie plan in place.

"All right, then. I'd splash them with water, like the Wicked Witch of the West."

My answer just made him hostile.

"If you're not going to be serious about this, we're not going to play." By this point he was so desperate for a smoke, he was trying to light a pencil in the toaster.

"Play? This is supposed to be fun?"

"No, I mean it, Mom. Smarten up or I'm not even going to talk to you."

"Really? You promise?"

I excused myself and put myself to bed before I did some serious damage. As I was drifting off to sleep, I heard a voice drifting up from the TV room.

"If you don't shut your mouth, I am going to stick a cigarette up your butt."

No, it was not an alien from another planet. It was the shrill sound of my daughter, who had just arrived home. She was screaming at her zombie-loving brother.

As they hissed back and forth — *Screw you! No, screw you!* — I thought, "Wow, it's great to hear the tittle-tattle of big people in the house."

The next day he bought the patch, keeping the Export As at bay. No zombies showed up unannounced, and I YouTubed Jane Jacobs, giving her 689 hits.

LETTING MY MOTHER LEAD

"you have to let the man lead,' she'd say, which i found crazy since most of the men were outside drinking by the truck."

As I was slow-dancing with my mother, I thought to myself that if someone had told me this is how life would look five years after my divorce, I might have stayed married.

My Dad was dead. My husband had been voted off the island. And my mother and I were at a seniors dance hall called The 39 Club. I thought it was named for people born in '39, but actually it was for people who wanted to pretend to be 39. I asked if I could tag along, because I wanted to see what the big attraction was.

When I asked her what I should wear, she said, "There is no point in wearing a push-up bra. We aren't there for any hanky-panky."

My mother shook her head and said, "Men are the same no matter what age they are. After your father died, they came out of the closet." I think she meant "woodwork." I was going to correct her and say if they came out of the closet, she had no need to be worried. But I didn't. As it turned out, the sniffers were far and few between. If you think there's poor selection at fifty, try eighty. It's like Grade Eleven but with age spots instead of acne. Besides, let's face it — most men don't dance. Sure, after a few cocktails you might get one to move up and down like he's pumping a well, but not many have mastered the art.

From an early age, I knew men were not necessary appendages for dancing. I was thirteen when my parents took me to Beaver Lake Pavilion (no double-entendre there — just the name of the lake next to the dance hall). The men stood outside in short-sleeved shirts shooting the breeze, while the women rocked it inside. I remember sipping lemon gin from a Wink bottle, watching my Mom's skirt flare out as she jived with her sisters. When the music slowed down, she'd try to teach me to two-step, but I always tried to lead. "You have to let the man lead," she'd say, which I found crazy since most of the men were outside drinking by the truck.

Flash forward to present day in The 39 Club. The band played dance music you needed a partner for, and because so many single women attended, they developed what they call "opportunity dances." During certain songs, the music would stop several times so men could ask the single women to dance.

My mother poked me in the ribs. "Target your man. Because when that music stops, the women get aggressive." Well, I'm not going to hip check an eighty-year-old woman so I can get asked to dance. She'd kick with her metal knee. Besides, I don't mean to sound picky, but I like a man without yellow toenails. As it turned out, when opportunity knocked, neither one of us got asked to dance. So I asked my mother if she wanted to kick it up old school, once around the room for old times' sake.

"All right," she said. "As long I get to lead."

As she pushed me across the dance floor like a janitor with a broom, I tried to tell her how much fun I was having. But she just stared off into space. Perhaps she was checking out the sniffer with the psychedelic walker giving her the eye. But more likely she hadn't heard me because she'd left her hearing aid in her purse.

THE DOCTOR'S ORIFICE

"i listen to people's medical problems only if i gave birth to them."

I was in need of a medical tune-up, so I called my doctor.

The receptionist said he could fit me in late in the afternoon. I thought it would be a quick visit. I would be put up on the hoist and be back on the road in short order. When I got there, the waiting room was full of the usual suspects: sick people and snotty kids pushing the hand sanitizer lotion button over and over again. There was also a guy with a fishhook in the side of his cheek. It was the opening day of walleye season, and his buddy had been behind him in the boat and hadn't cast quite far enough.

Fishhook Guy was flirting with Broken-Arm Woman. She didn't give him the time of day. Perhaps because she didn't find a man with a fishhook in his cheek attractive. Or perhaps because she was flirting with the Prisoner Man sitting beside her. She must not have seen Uniformed Escort because I heard her ask Prisoner Man, "Where are you from?" To which he replied, "A gated community."

As Broken-Arm Woman was called into the exam room, Prisoner Man winked at me. I averted my eyes. Not because I'm against dating a man in prison, it's just that I know if I smiled back, he'd start telling me about his medical problems. I listen to people's medical problems only if I gave birth to them. So I buried my head in an old magazine, a *Chatelaine* from the '70s with Helen Reddy on the cover. Although I pretended to be interested in how she wrote the song "I Am Woman," I couldn't help but be drawn into listening to the conversation between Fishhook Guy, Prisoner Man, and Uniformed Escort. Fishhook Guy started off saying he hates doctors. He sounded like my dad. My dad wouldn't go to the doctor either. He was a cowboy, a real *hombre*. He worked fixing up houses and when he came home from a job there'd be a big hunk of skin missing, and we'd ask, "Dad, where's your elbow?" He'd look down and say, "Oh God, I thought I was missing something."

Prisoner Man must have read my mind because he turned to me

and said, "Men are hunters. They don't like being vulnerable."

I was tempted to say federal prison would make you vulnerable, but I didn't because I wanted to stay out of it. I kept my head down and my mind wandered as I tried to recall statistics I heard when I took medicine at Queen's. Or was it when I took drugs at Queen's? Or maybe it was a conversation with somebody at the Queen's Hotel? I remember somebody telling me if a man is having a heart attack, he will deny it. He'll say, "Don't call 911. I just have a little indigestion." You can tell if a man actually does have indigestion. He'll burp in your face and say, "Sorry, babe."

The male psyche is confusing. A man says he's macho and doesn't want to be weak, but when that same man gets a sniffle, he'll be flattened on the couch unable to reach for the remote. Big babies with a man cold. No machismo, just a lot of coughing and hacking. I think that's why polygamy was never a woman's idea. No woman would ever get up one day and say, "Hey, I think I am going to get me seventeen husbands." That would be seventeen men who would get sick, likely all on the same day.

I read one study that said men find it hard to go the doctor because the waiting rooms are not male-friendly. Well, maybe we could decorate it like a hunting lodge? Put some moose heads on the wall? Or design the office like a mechanic shop? They could drive in, bend over the engine, and get their prostate checked and an oil change at the same time.

All of these thoughts were running around my brain when Prisoner Man winked at me again and said, "I guess women are used to being poked and prodded, so they're more comfortable at the doctor's than a man."

I looked at him and thought, *No wonder you're in jail. You likely said that to a female judge.* I smile and think, *Yes, man, you're right.* In fact, the week before, when the mammogram technician was twisting my left breast into a balloon animal, tightening the vice-grip device over what's left of my post-menopausal mammary, I thought to myself, *Whew, this is relaxing. Good thing I am not a man.*

Or a year before, when I had my feet up in the silver stirrups covered in oven mitts. The doctor entered with his miner's light and didn't even say hello. He said, "Scooch." Scooch is never a comfortable word for a woman. And it's not just the physical discomfort; it's the emotional discomfort. Why does he get all chatty when he's south of the border? Once he's got out the salad servers, he starts talking about his golf game. One time he said, "Oh, you've been to the beach."

He has no sense of timing. He's looking up Magic Mountain and said, "I see your tonsils are swollen." He had been looking at my throat ten minutes before, but he didn't say anything then. It was like he was a CNN news anchor reporting from Baghdad, where there is a time delay in his response.

So I shot back, "Can you see them from that angle?" He got embarrassed and said, "Uh no, I mean, well, I am an ear, nose, and throat man by trade, and I was just thinking…"

So no, going to the doctor is not comfortable for me, Prisoner Man. It's not comfortable for any of us, so suck it up. Act like a woman. During the yucky parts, lie back and think of England. A prison in England.

Of course, I didn't say this to Prisoner Man. I didn't know what he'd been in for. That, and the doctor was ready to see me now.

I went in. I got up on the table and put my feet in the stirrups with the oven mitts. The doctor came in and told me to scooch down a bit and began talking about shooting a ball into the rough while I lay there reading pithy cartoons on the ceiling, humming "I am woman, hear me roar."

CAT WITH A CAN ON ITS HEAD

"Wisdom isn't honoured in this society. there is no show called canada's next top crone."

Every winter we doubt spring will come.

But sure as anything, one morning we'll be wearing a hat and mitts and by afternoon we'll be wearing shorts and applying sunscreen. Climate change has made spring almost obsolete.

I love spring. Spring brings flower buds and new ideas and the bunny that brings candy. You have to admit, that's one fertility story that went horribly askew. I never really bought the idea of the Easter Bunny. Neither did my daughter. When she was about seven, she said to me, "Mommy, the Easter Bunny doesn't make sense. A rabbit couldn't hop around the world in one night delivering eggs."

I thought to myself, *This is a smart kid. She takes after my side of the family*. I was about to spill the jelly beans and tell her the whole truth, but within a split second she turned to me and said, "The rabbit would *definitely* need a magic chicken."

Of course he would. *Definitely*.

The point of this story is my daughter needed a magic chicken to get her through the winter and I needed a wild cat to bring me hope. Let me explain. Two years ago, I went through a long dark patch. I could call it a dark night of the soul, but really it was an entire season. Winter for a long, long time. Dark when you woke up, dark all day, and dark when you went to bed. Even my SAD light was depressed. My kids had left home. My marriage had ended. I was shaken to the core.

When your kids leave, it's called empty nest syndrome. Nowadays we need to call things syndromes so we can get a prescription. But having no man in your life? There is no medication for that, no patch you can purchase. In fact, all you get when your marriage ends is unsolicited advice. One camp says, "Don't worry! You'll find somebody." Another says, "You don't need anybody." Yet another group says, "Don't leave it too long." I guess we're like cars. We need to take them out for a spin or they'll seize up.

But then there are people like my friend Rachel, who said, "You are grieving. This is just loss — there's nothing wrong with you. In fact, there is a course you can take from a Buddhist temple in L.A. called 'There's Nothing Wrong with You.'"

I was reassured to think that I could pay to travel all the way to California to find out there's nothing wrong with me.

In the middle of this dilemma, the kicker was my dog had to be put down. Most people sigh a big horrible sigh when I say this. They are fine with the kids going and the man leaving, but the dog dying really gets to them. It got to me too. It was like I was trapped in a country and western song and I couldn't get out. I coped with it by making soup — pots and pots of soup. Containers upon containers of soup were lined up in my freezer, all in alphabetical order.

The only place I could keep it together was at work. I had to travel from hamlet to suburb being funny, and I realized I could turn on the charm for about as long as it took for the audience to clap and for me to collect the cheque and get to the car. But by the time I turned on the ignition, I'd be bawling again.

During this time I began talking to my cats, but I got nothing back. See, cats are a lot like drunks. They go out for three days and act like it's your fault that you expected them home for dinner. I often wondered *what is that cat thinking?* but anything that stands there picking at the fabric of the couch over and over again is not thinking about much. They are not ruminating. Cats have OCD.

One night I heard something banging on the door. I thought it was the cat that usually knocks on the door, but when I looked down it was standing right beside me. So I went outside and snuck around to the garage and when I looked in, I spied a grey ball of fur with a pink thing on its head. As I drew closer, I saw it had an empty cat food can stuck on its head. A wild cat had gotten into the garage and got its head stuck in a pink can of Mr. Whiskas, and it was freaking out. So I took a broom and tried to knock the can off, but it didn't help.

Then I called my neighbours and said, "I've a feral cat in my garage with a can on its head."

"Have you been drinking?" they asked.

"No, there is a cat with a can on its head and it's going to die."

"So what? It's a feral cat!" Amherst Island is crawling with them. So, after a few more attempts to get the can off, I concluded I would have to let it die.

I never wanted to be Dr. Quinn, Medicine Woman. I am not a character on "Little House on the Prairie." I was fifty-two and alone, and I didn't want to be that way. And oh, sure, I was older and wiser, but wisdom isn't honoured in this society. There is no TV show called "Canada's Next Top Crone." I didn't want to wear a red hat or go on a bus trip.

The next morning, I got up and got the shovel to bury the dang dead cat I knew would be waiting for me out in that garage. But when I opened the door there it was. Sitting there without a can on its head. I've never been so happy to see something alive — I looked at the cat and suddenly had an epiphany. I thought, *Life is like this. Sometimes we get a pink cat food can stuck on our heads and we run around trying to get it off but if we just relax, it's all okay.*

It may not sound like an *Aha!* moment but for me it was almost as grand as when Scrooge raced through the streets on Christmas Day yelling "Merry Christmas, one and all!" I was so filled with love for that blasted cat that I bent down and petted it.

And it scratched me to shreds, because that's what a wild cat does.

Then I went to the hospital because I thought I had cat scratch fever, and they gave me a tetanus shot and said, "Go on home. There is nothing wrong with you."

And I said, "I knew that." I went home and cancelled my flight to California.

So yes, winter ends, and spring comes in like a lamb or a lion. And the magic chicken helps the Easter Bunny get the chocolate delivered.

More importantly, that cat taught me two very important lessons. One: Always wash out cat food cans before you recycle them. And two: That which doesn't kill you makes you funnier.

ABOUT THE AUTHOR

Deborah Kimmett is an accomplished author (her two books are *Reality is Over-Rated* and *Outrunning Crazy*) and a Governor General's Award-nominated playwright. She's also a regular on CBC's "The Debaters" and a thirty-year veteran of The Second City. She tours North America as a motivational speaker helping people deal with change.

www.ingramcontent.com/pod-product-compliance
Lightning Source LLC
Chambersburg PA
CBHW051703090426
42736CB00013B/2524